# MORESHES BAIS YAAKOV SEMINARY
*A Brief Overview*

Founded in 1991, Moreshes Bais Yaakov Seminary proudly carries on the tradition of the Bais Yaakov movement to train future teachers. The program in education includes methodology, classroom observation and student teaching. The Torah Umesorah Teachers License awarded to the graduates attests to the solid pedagogic training available at Moreshes.

However, not all seminary graduates will enter the field of education. The growing role of women in helping to support their families, directs the urgent need for other options. Thus, in addition to Judaic subjects, Moreshes offers courses in marketable skills, including: accounting, computer science, creative writing and Special Education.

The unique Moreshes program and its beautiful country-like setting in the Torah community of Lakewood, New Jersey, have appealed to students from the local area. With the opening of a tastefully appointed dormitory, Moreshes has successfully attracted students from throughout the United States and from countries beyond, including Canada, Switzerland, Israel and the former U.S.S.R..

The staff of Moreshes is led by seasoned professionals. Rabbi Eli Lazar, founder and Dean, is a veteran Torah mechanech with over three decades of experience. The faculty is comprised of master teachers, each an expert in his or her field. The strategic location in the Torah citadel of Lakewood makes it possible to draw from a vast pool of talent for the Moreshes staff.

The Moreshes program has gained wide acceptance in the Torah world and is guided by the Rabbinic Va'ad of distinguished Roshei Yeshiva, HaRav Reuven Feinstein shlita, HaRav Shmuel Kamenetzky shlita and HaRav Malkiel Kotler shlita.

Moreshes has accomplished a great deal in the six short years of its existence; 147 young women have graduated the program since its inception and many alumnae have embarked upon careers in Jewish Education and Special Education. Others are employed in school and local offices utilizing the vocational skills acquired at Moreshes.

In February 1997, another major innovation in women's education was instituted by Moreshes. Thirty women embarked upon a fully-accredited program of courses in computers, accounting and Special Education. The new Moreshes Institute for Women is constantly developing new curricula which will build additional parnossa-generating skills.

Moreshes is still a young institution and it is crucial that it develop a strong base of founding supporters to help it implement its goals. You are invited to join and participate in the growth and development of Moreshes Bais Yaakov --- an innovator in traditional Jewish education.

Selected Readings from

# Shining LIGHTS

## Illuminating Stories of Faith and Inspiration

### Ruchoma Shain

FELDHEIM PUBLISHERS
Jerusalem / New York

First published 1997
Copyright © 1997 by Ruchoma Shain

All rights reserved.
No part of this publication may be
translated, reproduced, stored in a retrieval
system or transmitted, in any form or by any
means, electronic, mechanical, photocopying,
recording, or otherwise, without permission in
writing from the publishers.

FELDHEIM PUBLISHERS
POB 35002 / Jerusalem, Israel

200 Airport Executive Park
Nanuet, NY 10954

# Soul Mates

LEARN TO WAIT, Author unknown

Learn to wait — life's hardest lesson,
Conned, perchance, through blinding tears,
While the heartthrobs sadly echo
To the tread of passing years.
Learn to wait — hope's slow fruition;
Faint not, though the way seems long;
There is joy in each condition;
Hearts through suffering may grow strong.
Thus a soul untouched by sorrow
Aims not at a higher state;
Joy seeks not a brighter morrow;
Only wise hearts learn to wait.

Most of us have gone through periods in our lives in which we have had to wait for our hopes and dreams to be realized. This is especially so when one has to wait for a long time for the right marital match. This can be a difficult test, and only complete faith in Hashem can help one to accept this waiting period with peace of mind.

❋ ❋ ❋

"Mrs. Shain, are you sure that you want my story in your book?" Chava asked shyly.

I smiled. "Your story, Chava, is just the kind that will give readers encouragement and help them to see how Hashem takes care of each and every one of us." Chava reflected on the series of events that had taken place over fourteen years earlier. This is her story:

IT WASN'T AN EASY time for me, and I knew my relationship with Hashem was being put to the test. While I had learned that a person is never given a test that she can't handle, at that time I was not at all sure that I would get a passing mark. Nevertheless, what could I do? I had to find a *shidduch!*

It had been over a year since I had informed all the "right people" that I felt I was ready to get married and build a *bayis ne'eman b'Yisrael*. They had all agreed with me, which was encouraging, but I had begun to lose my optimism. I had always been a realistic person with reasonable doubts, and I took stock of the facts:

I was an American *ba'alas teshuvah* who had been in Israel for two-and-a-half years studying and now working part-time; I was average-looking; I had a university education; I was a self-supporting health professional; I was a little over the usual age for *shidduch*-seeking; and I walked with long leg braces and crutches, due to a childhood bout with polio.

Despite the first four points, the last two facts made the picture complicated. Although I was enthusiastic, sensitive, respected, and well-liked by my teachers, co-workers, neighbors, and friends, matchmakers were stumped. They listened respectfully to my analysis of the situation, and to my hopes for my "husband-to-be," and assured me I was not being unreasonable; yet, they let me know very tactfully that we all need a lot of *siyatta d'Shemaya* (Divine intervention) when it comes to *shidduchim*. This I understood very well.

The months went by, and not even one suggestion was presented to me. I tried to be patient, and I knew that when I would finally be introduced to a young man, at least I would meet someone who knew about me and was interested in meeting me for the stated purpose of marriage.

As I watched my roommates go out night after night, I could not help but feel neglected and rejected. At least, they had a hope that "this one" would be the right one. A Rebbetzin I knew, who was a matchmaker, tried to help. She was genuinely interested in trying to find the right person for me. There were a few suggestions from friends, but they certainly were not for me, and it seemed as if Hashem was keeping "him" hidden.

I even toyed with the idea of leaving Israel and returning to the States. Maybe my *zivug* was waiting for me over there! Most of the Rabbis I consulted advised me not to leave, however, so I stayed. The months went by. I was very busy with work, friends, studying, and concentrating intently on my prayers. The loneliness of those days and the uncertainty of my future tore at my very being.

During *chol ha-mo'ed* Pesach, I went on an organized trip to the Galilee, which included lunch at Lake Kinneret, and visiting the graves of the *tzaddikim* including the tomb of R. Yonason ben Uziel in Amukah, a site renowned for helping people find their *zivugim*. It was a glorious spring day and the scenery surrounding Amukah was breathtaking. The entire area was covered in lush green vegetation and the wildflowers, especially the bright, red poppies springing from the grass wherever you looked, blanketed the hills. The slowly setting sun completed the serenity of this holy place.

I will never forget those *Minchah* prayers. Though I stood amidst the others, I felt entirely alone with Hashem. My tears came easily, and mingled with my prayers. All the women in the group lingered there beyond sundown, feeling a unique connection with each other, and not wanting to disturb the harmony that surrounded us. Thinking of how many had stood there before with the same prayers, I had the comforting thought that Hashem's power and His loving-kindness were limitless and that we were all special in His eyes.

Six weeks later, the Rebbetzin told me she had met someone she thought would be worthwhile for me to meet, and that he was interested in meeting me. Her description of him sounded reasonable, and though I was very excited, I calmly agreed to meet Gedalya.

My roommates waited up for me after my first date, and I watched their excitement mount as they saw my smiling face. I went through five long days of anxiety waiting to hear if he was interested in seeing me again. What was taking so long??

Finally, the Rebbetzin called and assured me that he wanted to see me again. Over the loud pounding of my heart, a small voice inside whispered, "Thank you, Hashem."

Our following meetings were intense and lively. It was so comfortable to just be myself, even though I was sleeping less and praying more! I knew it was getting serious, and I wrote my parents about him. They were very excited too.

What is it that enables a person to know that this *shidduch* is the one? Of course, every person is different, but I believe that one has to know and understand herself first. Self-awareness had been a way of life for me for years. Growing up with a disability presented so many challenges that I learned very early that successful problem-solving came from an honest awareness of one's self and others. My parents taught me this simply through experience. I felt that my husband-to-be would not only have to have certain strengths and sensitivities, but also that I would have to see them before saying "Yes!"

Hashem showed me the signs. I experienced one situation after another which enabled me to see how Gedalya would act in emergencies, and react to my dilemmas and weak moments. The entire picture became brighter and clearer to me, and the final resolve came in a very unexpected but natural way.

We planned a picnic in a park which had a lovely little lake. There were rowboats for rent there. "Let's go rowing," I suggested. Gedalya looked at me with some surprise and a certain amount of trepidation. "Do you really want to?" he asked. "Sure," I said confidently, realizing, as I saw the rickety rowboat that this would not be so simple. Under my confident exterior, I was thinking, "I must not become a spectacle. I must get myself into this boat in a graceful manner." The area was fairly empty, so at least I did not have to perform in front of any audience. Still I wondered what he was thinking as I casually suggested how he could steady the boat while I climbed in. I slowly and carefully stepped into the rickety boat, silently praying that I would not fall into the lake or embarrass either of us in some other clumsy way. I did it! Nothing to it, I thought, as I tossed my crutches into the back of the boat and sat down with a sign of relief. Little did I know then that he was more worried about remembering how to row a boat and impress me with his navigational skills than he was about whether I would manage. Being human is such a wonderful thing!!

As we went home on the bus together, I knew I had to ask Gedalya the question that had been on my mind: "How did the Rebbetzin present the idea of meeting me, and what made you decide to agree?"

He answered frankly. "The Rebbetzin did not mention you personally, but she asked me, in her own careful way, what I would think about going out with someone with a physical disability. I told her that I'd never thought about it, but that I would do so and let her know. She said that it was important for her to know, in case such a situation presented itself.

"I decided to go to the *Kosel*," he continued, "and as I stood there, deep in prayer and reflection, I realized that the most essential aspect of a marriage partner was that person's soul, and that one's outer self was certainly secondary to the inner self. I then told the Rebbetzin that I was looking for a special person, and external things, hopefully, would not prevent me from recognizing her when I met her. It was then that she told me about you."

I was so touched by what he told me that I was at a loss for words. The last years flashed through my mind — the lonely evenings, the uncertainties, the friends trying to help me, the advice of the Rabbis, and the visit to Amukah.... I said a prayer to Hashem: "Blessed is God, Who has not turned away my prayer nor His kindness from me" (*Tehillim* 66:20). I had found the person I was looking for. We were married two months later.

Chava and Gedalya have remained in Jerusalem, and with Hashem's help are raising their four children to love and trust Hashem and to appreciate the inner essence of each person.

❈   ❈   ❈

DORY WAS A well-adjusted, happy eighteen-year-old when she was introduced to Philip, who was two years older. She had just graduated from Bais Yaakov high school, and though she felt she was a bit young for marriage, there were such glowing reports about Philip and his family, that her parents encouraged her to meet him.

After several meetings, they became engaged. Since Dory had found him to be such a fine young man, she could not understand why, the night of the engagement party, she suddenly felt unsure about the match. However, her parents were very happy with him and felt that he would be like a new son. As the wedding day approached, Dory continued to have many misgivings, but somehow she could not bring herself to disappoint her parents, who were very excited and in the midst of wedding plans.

After their marriage, Dory and Philip moved to a different city, which was very far from her parents and family. Within a few months, she began to acknowledge Philip's strange behavior, and realized that he was not conducting himself as a Torah Jew should. Her original doubts about him came back, but she was wary about confronting him, so she let the issues pass.

In her letters and telephone calls to her parents, she could not tell them what was going on, and they continued to think that he was very special. The few times they visited her parents, Philip put on such a show of being the perfect husband and pious Jew that she just could not disillusion them.

When they had been married for almost two years, Dory decided that she could no longer continue the farce, and she telephoned her parents and told them that she was coming home and would explain everything when she got there. She packed up some of her clothes, and went to the airport, and was able to get a flight without too much waiting. She had left a note for Philip telling him that she was leaving.

Her parents were waiting for her at the airport, puzzled and distraught.

A year later, she received her religious and civil divorce, which he did not contest.

For the first time since she had met Philip, Dory found peace of mind. However, the stigma of being a divorced woman at the age of twenty-one was something she had to live with. She was encouraged to start dating again, but none of the young men she met were suitable. Dory was very wary and fearful of going into an unsuccessful marriage a second time.

Several years passed, and she tried her best to be patient and to believe that Hashem would answer her many prayers and send her the right one, but it was not easy for Dory. After her divorce, she had been advised to not wear her wig, as it might detract from her chances for marriage. When she applied for a teaching position in a very reputable, religious girls' school, however, the principal, who had heard that she had been married before, insisted that she wear a wig. Dory sought the advice of a prominent rabbi, who told her to start wearing a wig, and blessed her that Hashem would help her find her true *zivug* very soon.

She followed his advice, although it meant advertising to all that she had been married before and was divorced. A few months later she was introduced to Chaim, a fine young man, who also had gone through a very unhappy first marriage. It did not take long for Dory to realize that Chaim was the husband she had been looking for, and for him to feel that Dory was what he had hoped for in a wife.

Their marriage has been a most loving and happy one, and their children are growing up in a home that is filled with love and security, with Torah as their guide. Dory told me, "I think that Hashem answered my prayers, because I immediately accepted the advice of the rabbi to wear a wig. This was not easy; it was really a test of faith for me. And *baruch Hashem*, both Chaim and I value our relationship so much more because of the suffering we both had to withstand before."

❦ ❦ ❦

I was attending a wedding when Karen came over and introduced herself. "Mrs. Shain, I understand you are writing a new book and are interested in special experiences. I think I have one that you might find suitable." Karen's story goes back many years, and happened in the United States, before her family moved to Israel.

I WAS BUSY IN THE kitchen, when I heard a sudden commotion and a woman burst into my apartment, which was on the ground floor. "Quick, call the police, call an ambulance!" she cried. "A girl has been run over, and she's hurt very badly." I immediately called an ambulance and then went out to the street to see what had happened.

A crowd had already gathered around the teenage girl, who lay unconscious. She had been crossing the street, and a speeding car had hit her and sped away. When the ambulance arrived, the doctor pronounced her dead.

I looked at her lying there so helpless, and thought about the fragility of life. When I made inquiries about the girl, I was told that Miriam was a religious seventeen-year-old and had been attending a seminary not far from where she was killed. She had been on her way to get the bus home when the speeding driver had hit her. I decided to make a *shivah* call to her parents, and though I had not known Miriam personally, the sorrow of her death touched me deeply and I cried with her parents and family.

For many weeks afterwards, I was depressed and could not get Miriam's face out of my mind. I tried to keep busy with various activities, but I could not find peace of mind. Finally, my husband, Saul, spoke to his Rebbe about my problem.

Saul explained to him what had occurred, and my emotional reaction to it, which did not allow me peace of mind. Saul asked the Rebbe if I should perhaps undertake to help the new Russian immigrants who had recently arrived in our community, but the Rebbe did not respond. He then asked the Rebbe if I should perhaps get involved with guidance counseling to help troubled teenagers, something I'd done in the past, but again the Rebbe did not respond. Saul remembered that I'd once told him how I'd like to sort of try my hand at matchmaking, so he asked the Rebbe about that possibility. Immediately the Rebbe replied, "Yes, that's it!" He sent Saul home with a blessing that I be successful in making a *shidduch*.

A week later, a former teacher of mine mentioned that her neighbor had a very fine son who would like to meet a special girl. Because of the Rebbe's advice, I decided to pursue this *shidduch*. I contacted the young man's mother and arranged to meet her son, Zelig. "What are you looking for in a wife?" I asked him. He did not hesitate, and answered quickly, "I would like a girl who is modest and careful with her speech." I immediately thought about Hindy, with whom I was very close. Just a few weeks earlier she had been our Shabbos guest and had told me that she was trying to improve two traits of hers before Rosh Hashanah — being more modest and watching what she says. I told Zelig that I thought I might have the special girl he was looking for.

Zelig and Hindy met, got engaged a short while later, and married within six months. After her marriage, Hindy visited me quite often and told me how happy she was with Zelig. One afternoon, she confided in me that she was expecting a baby. "Tell me," she said. "I've often wondered: How did you get involved in my *shidduch*?"

I told her about the experience I had gone through, and the Rebbe's advice, which had led to my meeting Zelig. I went on to tell her that when he said he was interested in a girl who was modest and careful with her speech, of course I had thought of her, since she had expressed these same sentiments to me a few weeks earlier. Hindy did not say anything, but when their baby girl was born, she and Zelig decided to name her after Miriam, *z"l*, who had really been the person who had brought them together. They added the name Bracha — "a blessing" — to Miriam.

I decided to visit Miriam's parents and tell them the story, and that Zelig and Hindy's daughter had been named after their Miriam. They listened and wept softly and then Miriam's mother said to me, "We can see Hashem's Guiding Hand in all this, for Miriam, *z"l*, was always especially careful in her speech and modest in her dress."

Zelig and Hindy are praying that their Bracha Miriam have the same sterling qualities as the girl for whom she was named.

❀ ❀ ❀

I became very friendly with Sonia after she and her father moved into our apartment building in Jerusalem. Her father was on a Sabbatical leave from an American university, where he was a professor. This is Sonia's story:

WHEN MY FATHER was fifty years old, he quite suddenly suffered a massive heart attack, which was almost fatal. He survived, *baruch Hashem*, but was left with 50% heart function. This caused him to change his life completely. He returned to the Jewish tradition of his childhood, where he was raised by a religious mother and grandparents. When he was released after a month's hospitalization, he checked into a yeshiva in Brooklyn, began to study Torah, and became a true *ba'al teshuvah*.

He liked to point out to us that the damage was mostly on the left side of his heart and that *Kabbalah* associates the animal side of our nature with the left side, while our Godly part is associated with the right. At the time of my father's transformation, I was fifteen years old, and at the peak of my rebellious years. It seemed to me that he had become a complete stranger, with his long black beard and the "strange" things he said. Though he was the same loving, devoted father, these new values were completely foreign to me. My parents had raised me on atheism, and I had no knowledge of any God or Jewish tradition.

As a matter of fact, my father had always been different from my friends' fathers! He always threw himself into his beliefs, and didn't care what others thought about him. At the height of the McCarthy era, he was an outspoken Communist and was quoted in *Time* magazine as saying, "Krushchev (President of the Soviet Union) is like a father to me" — much to the horror and embarrassment of his parents. In his college years, he traveled to Russia and China, and his passport was confiscated by the FBI; those were the Cold War years and fear of Communist spies was rampant.

My father eventually grew disenchanted with Communism, and tried extreme left-wing Zionism for a while. Then he discovered Freudian psychoanalysis, with his usual passion and enthusiasm, but ultimately found that also to be lacking what his soul was searching for. It was at that point that my parents divorced. Shortly afterwards he suffered his heart attack and returned to Judaism.

I stayed with my father, and kept a kosher home as best I could, even though I steadfastly kept far away from other aspects of his Torah observance.

When we came to Israel, I was looking forward to spending the year on a kibbutz, which I saw as a utopian ideal, but I was soon disappointed and discouraged when I discovered that the other young people on the kibbutz I went to were just as depressed as I was from the empty values of our secular world.

I returned to stay with my father in the small apartment he had rented in Jerusalem. Hashem was watching over him, and he became friendly with the Rabbis who lived in the building. During his first week, he met Mrs. Shain and told her how inspired he had been by her book, *"All for the Boss."* My father asked her if she could try to influence his daughter — and since she was giving weekly classes in a seminary, she invited me to attend them. That's how it happened that every Monday morning we took the bus together to the seminary.

I became very inspired by her down-to-earth lectures, and by my fellow classmates, who were highly educated young women from the secular world who had recently returned to Jewish tradition and undertaken to follow the path of Torah. I began to understand, finally, the world my father had come back to, a world I had never known existed.

Now, to go back a number of years — when I was fourteen,

Bobby, a Jewish boy who was several years older than I, had become my friend and companion. When my father and I came to Israel, he had phoned us long distance every Sunday morning. He told me that he wanted to visit us in Israel when he graduated. Now, though, I did not want to continue my relationship with him, since my life had taken on a completely different direction.

My father, however, saw things in a different light. "Look," he said, "if you saw a person lost in a maze, you would surely try to rescue him, wouldn't you?" My father spoke to some of the rabbis who were involved in outreach work and asked them to interest themselves in Bobby when he came. I met him at the airport and an hour later he was surprised to find himself sitting in a very prominent seminary for men who were becoming *ba'alei teshuvah*.

It took Bobby a few weeks to figure out what had hit him, but the wisdom and clarity of what he was learning began to sink in. When he compared the secular and competitive academic world he came from with the Torah world that was being revealed to him, he realized that he had been a lost soul. He decided to observe Shabbos and *kashrus*, put on *tefillin*, and wear *tzitzis*. He was particularly moved by hearing me make blessings on all the food I ate. He had always had a sensitivity and appreciation of the world around him, but was never taught how to express that appreciation until he came into contact with authentic Jewish life.

Bobby (now known as Baruch) spent his five-month winter semester at the yeshiva, and then returned to the States shining with the glow of Torah. We were married the next fall after he finished university. We returned to Israel almost two years later with our three-month old daughter, and Baruch has made Torah study his full-time occupation.

Our joy was marred by my father's death a month before our wedding. I realized that he had been the messenger from

Heaven who brought Baruch and me back to Torah, and I hope that he is reaping his just reward in Heaven.

Although we will never forget my father, *z"l*, we are consoled by our five "shining lights" — our three daughters and two sons, who, God willing, will continue to follow in my father's legacy and inspire generations to come.

❉   ❉   ❉

Many of my readers contact me when they come to Jerusalem, and so it was with Rachel, who called and asked if she could visit me, having read my books. I enjoyed the visit with her immensely, for her story was so unusual and inspiring. I am presenting the stories of Rachel and her husband Irving separately.

### RACHEL'S STORY

I WAS BORN IN Cincinnati, Ohio, in 1951. My parents were both from Poland and my father is a concentration-camp survivor. I am the oldest of four children, and we grew up in a very traditional Jewish home. We kept kosher, with separate meat and milk dishes and utensils, and attended an Orthodox synagogue. However, we did not really keep Shabbos, although my mother lit candles, we had Friday night dinner together, and in the morning we walked to the synagogue which was close to our home.

By the time I was a teenager, I had stopped following these traditions, as the shul had moved further from us and I was only one of the four Jewish pupils in my public school. I began to stop keeping kosher, but I did go to shul — by car — on Shabbos. It was then that I left home for college and then to veterinary school, and ultimately to Columbus, Ohio, to work in veterinary research at Ohio State University.

The turning point in my life came when I almost married the wrong man. I became engaged on January 1, 1985, when I was thirty-four years old. That same day, I was in an automobile accident; my car was almost destroyed and, miraculously, I was only shaken up but not hurt. I remember saying to the doctor who examined me afterwards, "You know, I just got engaged today." I wondered at the time if this was some sign that I should heed, but I disregarded the thought.

That summer, my closest friend told me she was going to try to keep kosher. Although my mother had always advised me to wait until I got married and then have separate sets of dishes, it made more sense to me to start now also. What was I waiting for? When I told my fiancé that I wanted to keep kosher, he said, "Sure, you can keep kosher" — but as the date of our wedding, August 25, drew near, it dawned on me that he had no intention of keeping kosher himself. When I confronted him, he confirmed this, saying that I could do whatever I pleased, but he was still going to bring home his *traif* sausage pizzas!

This was but one difference in our views on Jewish observance. I began to realize that his idea of being Jewish was very different from mine. Whereas I wanted to grow in my Judaism, he did not. We consulted many people, including Rabbis, about this problem, but our differences remained. One week before the wedding, when my aunt and uncle had already arrived from Israel to attend the "simcha," my fiancé and I decided to postpone the wedding. Neither of us had the courage to cancel it at that point. My aunt was terribly disturbed, as she had been brought up to believe that Jewish weddings are not postponed. Many of our relatives and friends were sure that I just had pre-marital jitters, that I was too set in my ways, and I did not know how to compromise after being independent for so many years. But my gut feeling told me that my fiancé was not the right one for me, and after several weeks, we finally canceled the wedding and ended our relationship.

I decided to make a list of the things I wanted in the person I would marry. My list contained thirteen items, mostly Jewish and spiritual criteria. If I found such a man, I told myself, it would be wonderful, but if not, I simply would not get married. At that point, I also made a decision to start going again to an Orthodox shul. I decided to begin on Rosh Hashanah.

On the first day of the holiday, I went to a small Orthodox shul which had been recommended to me by a friend. He thought that I would respect the Rabbi and be able to consult with him about religious issues. Most of the congregants were very old people, but there was one young woman in the women's section, and I sat down next to her. When it came time for *Tashlich*, we walked together. As we left shul, it began to rain. She was wearing a beautiful new sweater, and I thought it would be such a shame to get it wet, so I took off my jacket and told her to put it on. At the evening service, she introduced me to her husband, who was the Cantor for the High Holidays.

Over the next few weeks, we became friends and just before Thanksgiving, she called and asked me if I would be interested in meeting her husband's brother, Irving, who lived in Memphis, Tennessee, and was planning to come up to Columbus to visit them. I had been planning to spend the four-day Thanksgiving weekend visiting my parents in Cincinnati, but I told her I might be able to meet him at the airport before my plane left at 5:00 PM. She said she would ask him when he was arriving, and see if it was possible. "I have to call him anyway," she added, "to wish him 'Happy Birthday' today." "Today is also my birthday!" I exclaimed, and then added, "I think I would like to meet your brother-in-law."

It worked out that I was able to meet Irving for an hour at the airport before my flight left. (At that time, neither of us realized that this was the typical Orthodox way to meet!) After this one brief meeting, I felt that he might be the right person for me, and I told my parents that I had met someone I liked. It was only three months since I had canceled my wedding and I did not want to get their hopes up, but still I was optimistic.

It turned out that we did not meet again until the beginning of March, and then we started our long-distance dating through telephone conversations and letters a few times a week. In retrospect this was a great way to get to know each other, as it did not put us under any pressure. We met again at Pesach, and afterwards we met about every three weeks. While we were dating, Irving confided in me that he had been a little skeptical about meeting a veterinarian (a lady who wrestles with cows, he imagined) who attended an old folks' shul. However, when his sister-in-law told him that I had been very thoughtful and had given her my jacket so that her new wool sweater would not get spoiled by the rain when we had gone to *Tashlich*, he was touched by this kind gesture. We were engaged in July and married the following December.

By almost marrying the wrong man, I realized what my values really were, and what I wanted out of life: to return to my Judaism and observe the mitzvos. I wanted to marry someone who would help me reach my Jewish potential and not stifle it. I had made a plan to start all over again on Rosh Hashanah, and Hashem, with His Divine Providence, sat me down in shul next to my future sister-in-law. Thank God that I went to that shul on Rosh Hashanah.

I did *teshuvah*, not really knowing at that time what the word meant. I could hear Hashem saying, "I accept your *teshuvah*, and now you are ready to meet the man you have been waiting for all your life."

I had to live through the terrible ordeal of a last-minute wedding cancellation with the wrong man, but it brought me to marry the right man.

Irving's moving story starts where Rachel's ends:

I WAS BORN IN 1953, the second of three sons. My parents were both Holocaust survivors from Poland. I grew up in Iowa City, Iowa, where there was one synagogue and one Reform temple. We kept kosher, but were not particularly *shomrei Shabbos*. My parents had a clothing store and worked there on Shabbos, but they insisted that we children go to shul. We were also sent to a Hebrew school twice a week after public school, but the teaching was on a low level. My father also insisted that we learn how to *daven*, but we had very little real knowledge of Jewish law or philosophy. I guess I was a pretty good "Jewish technician," but with no knowledge of or feeling for real Judaism. I studied medicine and became a cardiologist.

I was 33 years old when Rachel and I married and we set up our home in Memphis. When almost a year had passed and Rachel had not become pregnant, she went to a gynecologist and underwent a series of tests. When the results showed everything was fine with her, the doctor suggested that I do the same. As we were driving to a weekend retreat sponsored by our shul, Rachel broke the news to me that my tests showed that it would be highly improbable for me to father a child. We were both very depressed during the entire weekend.

I then saw a specialist who repeated some of the tests, and again they showed the same results. Rachel and I began to consider other alternatives, and we discussed the subject with our Rabbi, who felt that we could still have our own child. He told us that he had given our names to a *tzaddik*, who was praying for us. He suggested that Rachel wear a necklace with certain charms. He also advised me to eat certain foods, and since we felt that we had nothing to lose, we followed his advice, but nothing happened.

We consulted fertility experts about alternative methods, but whatever we attempted was not successful. Of course, there was adoption, but we were not ready for that. We heard that being given honors at a bris ceremony was a special *segulah* for conceiving, so many of our friends and my brother gave us those honors.

I heard that there was a convention of the American Urological Association scheduled in Memphis, on male infertility, and that international infertility experts would be there. As a physician, I registered and went to listen to the experts myself. I presented my situation to a few of them, as if it were one of my patient's, and they had nothing to offer. The facts were very discouraging, and this seemed like the final nail in the coffin for our hopes. Both Rachel and I had exhausted every avenue, and I was now absolutely certain that there was nothing else that we could do. We would, hopefully, have a child, but it would surely not be our own.

At that time, Rachel was not feeling well, and seemed fatigued a lot of the time. I dared to hope that maybe she was pregnant, and I privately made a deal with Hashem that if Rachel were pregnant, we would move to within walking distance of the shul, and I would become more involved in my Torah studies.

A short time later, I encouraged Rachel to take a pregnancy test and it was positive! At that moment, I was struck as if by lightning: Not only is there a God, I realized, but He is actually involved in the world, and He is actually directly involved with me!! Until that point, I had believed that there was a God Who created the universe, but I never seriously thought that He was involved in the minute details of each individual's life. But here it was! What was virtually physically impossible had happened, and I could not deny it.

That was my great moment of *teshuvah*. I realized immediately that if Hashem were indeed involved actively in the world and knew precisely what was going on in my life, then I had better take very seriously the mitzvos that He had given me and expected me to keep. Rachel was a bit surprised when I told her that we had to sell our house immediately and find a new house very close to our shul — something she had wanted us to do when we were first married.

Rachel's pregnancy went well, and a healthy daughter, Hadassa Nisya, our miracle from God, came into the world. Since then, *baruch Hashem*, we have been blessed with three more healthy children.

We don't know why Hashem singled us out, among so many infertile couples, to be blessed with children, but we are truly grateful and try to live our lives doing what He expects of us.

❦ ❦ ❦

When I received a letter from Shoshana, a former student, I was very pleased for I had told her that I was interested in hearing of any experiences of hers that would be suitable for my book. She enclosed the following:

A NUMBER OF YEARS ago when I was studying in a religious seminary in which most of the women were in their middle or late twenties, a new student from Europe arrived and entered our dormitory. Margalit had been in a tragic accident, a fire, a few years before, that left her scarred a bit on her face and her arms, and slightly lame in one leg. We could see that she had been a very attractive girl before this had happened.

Of course, all the students tried to make her feel comfortable, and we treated her with the usual warmth and friendship that characterized our seminary. It soon became clear, however, that the fire had scarred her not only physically, but emotionally as well. Every overture of ours was rebuffed, and every acerbic comment she made showed how bitter she was about life. When we realized that we could not develop any sort of relationship with Margalit, we all kept our distance, and she remained in her own shell.

It was towards the end of the school year, when one day we were very surprised to see a large note on our bulletin board inviting all the dormitory students to Margalit's engagement party the next evening. It was to be held in the home of a prominent Rebbetzin who was affiliated with our school. We had noticed that during the last few weeks Margalit had been missing classes often, and that she returned to the dormitory quite late at night, but we had never questioned her about her whereabouts.

Needless to say, we all were very excited by this turn of events. When we arrived at the engagement party, we were greeted by a completely different Margalit, who was warm and friendly. She introduced us to her *chasan* very proudly, and we noticed that he wore hearing aids in both ears, but that didn't keep him from having a friendly conversation with us. Several rabbis spoke at the party lauding both the *chasan* and *kallah*, who glowed with happiness.

From that night on, there was an amazing transformation in Margalit, who blossomed like a budding flower. We all became her close friends, sharing her joy in her approaching marriage. She was a beautiful, glowing bride with a radiant smile as she walked to the *chuppah*. As she circled her *chasan* seven times, her limp was not noticeable at all.

As I walked back to the dormitory after the wedding, I felt suddenly and clearly that I had witnessed the Hand of Hashem. I was in my late twenties, and I turned my face up to the heavens and prayed with all my heart, "*Ribbono shel Olam*, if you could make this miracle for Margalit, send me my *zivug*, too. I will try to make my house a bastion of Torah and *hachnasas orchim*, so that Your light will penetrate every corner of my home."

One month later I met my husband-to-be!

* * *

Shoshana's second experience took place a few years later, after she had given birth to her first child.

WHEN I HEARD that Beverly, a former classmate of mine, was seriously ill, I went to visit her. Perhaps I could cheer her up a bit, I thought. Beverly had been a brilliant student and a girl with a strong character, I recalled. She had not married, so I tried to think about what I could say that would help her in her difficult situation.

I took my year-old son along in his stroller and we set out. Although Beverly greeted me warmly and asked me about myself, I could see that she was so ill that it was probably a strain for her to talk. I told her that I was trying to build a home of Torah and *Yiddishkeit*, and that I hoped that my son and any other children I would have, would follow in that path. She was silent for a few minutes and then suddenly said, with a show of strength in her voice, "Remember, Shoshana, that nothing is permanent except Hashem, His Torah, and His mitzvos." Although I knew that she was right, I left feeling depressed, feeling that I had not cheered her up at all. Several months later, Beverly passed away.

The years sped by and life was busy for me as my family grew. When my sixth child was born, despite the normal birth, she had trouble breathing, and for almost a week, she fought desperately to live. My husband and I prayed for her life with all our hearts, but her precious, pure soul was returned to Hashem.

My pain at her loss was so intense that I could not function properly for a long time afterwards. One day, after the children had left for school, I opened my *siddur* to pray and suddenly, Beverly's words of so many years before returned to me full force. "Nothing is permanent except Hashem, His Torah, and

His mitzvos." I felt an intense closeness to Hashem, and wondered why we are closer to Him when we are in pain than when we are in pleasure.

A great sense of peacefulness came over me as I finally accepted His decree, and returned to my life with renewed faith that Hashem is my comfort, and the hope of my future and the future of my family.

I had met Pearl once, seven years earlier, when she was visiting Israel with a tour group from Canada, and had come to see me.

Her letter intrigued me, especially as I read that she wanted her story told because, as she wrote, "In our religious circles, I find that the aftermath of divorce and remarriage is hardly mentioned at all. If my experience will help to encourage couples in the same situation as mine and Mendy's, in building a true Jewish home and overcoming the difficulties of step-parenting, then it will be worth having my story told." Pearl wrote:

> Dear Mrs. Shain,
>
> I have been remiss in not writing this letter much sooner. I wonder if you remember me. It has been nearly seven years since I visited you and asked you to autograph my copy of *"All for the Boss."* When I met you, and saw how friendly you were, I asked you how I should go about trying to find a *shidduch* for myself. At the time, I was twenty-nine and despondent about ever finding my true mate.
>
> I had outlined a long list of requirements that I was looking for in a husband and I read the list to you: nice appearance, tall, in his thirties, financially secure, studying Torah

at night and working during the day....

I remember so clearly your suggestions:

1. Give up your long list of requirements! It is much too confining.

2. Ask your friends and even *shadchanim* to recommend suitable young men for you to meet.

3. Since you are in Israel, try to go to Amukah, the tomb of the great sage, Rabbi Yonason ben Uziel, and pray there. I have heard that many have been helped to find their true partners within a year of visiting his grave.

I took your advice, and within a year after I had gone to Amukah, I became a *kallah*. I also followed your advice about expectations and realities of *shidduchim*, which proved correct, and I thanked Hashem that I'd had the opportunity to meet you.

Now I would like to share with you the story of how I met my husband, Mendy. A close friend suggested him and told me about his very fine qualities. I was interested, of course, until she added that he was divorced and was raising two very young children. I was upset and hurt that she would think I would want to marry a man who had been divorced, not to mention the two children, which meant that I would have to be a step-mother!

I told her in no uncertain terms that I was definitely not interested. For some reason, however, I decided to discuss it with my parents and my Rabbi, who made inquiries about him and heard very good reports. They encouraged me to meet him, but I was not convinced. For three stressful weeks I mulled over the problem, and then I recalled what you said about not confining myself to my set of requirements — and I decided to meet him.

After several meetings, it was clear to me that Mendy was just the perceptive and sensitive person I was waiting for, and so we were married. Our marriage has been a successful one, and Mendy has been very supportive of me through the many ups and downs of being a step-mother.

Being a full-time step-mother to two very active children who were four and six at the time of our marriage has been fraught with many difficulties, and I have shed many tears. Time and time again, I prayed to Hashem to help me through the difficulties that overwhelmed me. During the six years of our marriage, I have also given birth to three of my own children, which taxed me physically and emotionally.

At the beginning, I sought counseling on how to deal with children who were "not my own," until I finally came to the realization that Mendy's children were indeed my own. Now Zissie is twelve and Benjie is ten and my three children range in ages from five years to fourteen months. They all relate to each other as true brothers and sisters of one big happy family.

Our lives are full, and we are busy parents who pray that Hashem will continue to give us the insight, strength and humor to raise our five children.

I would like to thank you again, Mrs. Shain, for our two-hour meeting that changed the course of my life.

> In deep appreciation,
> Pearl

❀ ❀ ❀

I started this chapter with the poem "Learn to Wait," and I am ending it with Chana's experience, which she calls: "It Paid to Wait."

I WAS EIGHTEEN years old when I went out on a *shidduch* date for the first time. I was already twenty-eight when I married. The ten intervening years were by no means easy, and there were times when I thought that my true *zivug* would never appear.

I prayed, I cried, and went to *tzaddikim* for blessings, and I asked all my friends to help me find the "right one." But the years went by, and I was twenty, and twenty-four, twenty-five, twenty-seven...and still not married. "Why?" I asked. "What does Hashem want from me?"

I often poured out my heart to Mrs. Shain, for we had grown very close to each other, and she always gave me the same answer: "Chana, we can't ask questions, because there are not always answers down here, and there won't be any questions 'up there.' But I do feel that one day you'll tell me, 'It paid to wait.'" I tried to take comfort in her words, but I could not imagine that I'd ever be *happy* that I had to wait so long for my true *zivug*.

Now I have been married for two-and-a-half years to my dear husband, Gershon Severe, and we have, *baruch Hashem*, two beautiful children, a son, Simcha, and a daughter, Orah. As I look at my children, I have finally understood why I had to wait, and I can say with all my heart, "Yes, it paid to wait."

I realized that Simcha and Orah had to be born at the time destined by Hashem, and not ten years or five years before. Hashem knew that I would have the strength to wait for my true partner in life, but that having to wait for many years for my children's birth would have been a test much too difficult to bear.

Those who have to wait can take comfort in the knowledge that Hashem does what is best for us, even though at the time we cannot always fathom His Infinite Mercy.

# Deliverance from Heaven

IN YOUR LIGHT WE SEE LIGHT. (TEHILLIM 36:10)

"I think that my story might be appropriate for your new book, Mrs. Shain," my caller told me in a cheerful British accent.

When Millie entered my home, I could see she was expecting a baby, and that she was considerably older than the average expectant mother. She told me that she now resides in Switzerland, but was born in London and lived there until a few years ago. This is Millie's story:

WHEN I WAS almost twenty years old, I met a young man who was a few years older than me and had a strong Jewish background very similar to mine. We seemed very suited to each other, as we had the same values and goals, and we married after a short courtship. For several years after our marriage, he studied in a *kollel*, and then joined his father in the family business. As with every Jewish couple, we looked forward eagerly to building a family, and I hoped that we would be blessed with many children.

However, as the years went by, our hopes for having children dimmed. Of course, I went to doctors and specialists, and none could find a medical problem. The next step, I was told, was that my husband should undergo tests.

Well, I decided to tell my husband only that they could find no problem with me. I did not — could not, somehow — add that the problem might be with him, but I was sure that he would understand that himself and take appropriate steps. I imagine that he did go to a doctor, but he never mentioned anything to me, and I held my silence.

Except for the deep disappointment and pain over not having children, we had a happy marriage and I accepted the situation. I was working as a school secretary, which kept me busy and gave me the opportunity to be in the close presence of children.

Twenty years passed, and one day my husband announced that he wanted a divorce. I had no idea who had advised him to do this, but I was sure that he had not come to the decision hastily. He did not give me any explanations, and, of course, I was very distraught, but I accepted it. Although we parted on good terms, I was left depressed.

Several months later, my parents suggested that I take a needed vacation and visit relatives in Switzerland. I took their advice, and my cousins there welcomed me warmly. Shortly after I arrived, one of my cousins suggested that I meet a man whose wife had passed away a year before. Meir was my age, and had three teenage children. He was a fine man, she said, well-liked in the community, and the principal of a Hebrew day school. I wasn't sure that I'd be able to be a good step-mother to three teenagers, but nevertheless, I felt that I should go ahead and meet Meir. We met several times, and got along very well. I could see he was a fine person and I liked him. When I met his children, two boys and a girl, I saw that it would not be easy to build a relationship with them. They had recently lost their beloved mother and they were at a difficult age as well, but with the encouragement and emotional support of my family, I accepted his proposal.

It meant a complete change in my life. I would have to live in Switzerland, where Meir's school was, and I would have to give up the job which I'd had for years and enjoyed very much. The role of step-mother still weighed heavily on my mind. But I was happy, and we had a small wedding in London.

A few months later, I began to feel quite ill, and when I went to the doctor, I could hardly believe my ears: I was expecting a baby! My husband was delighted, and when we told the children, they became much closer to me and tried to be very helpful. On our first anniversary, I gave birth to a beautiful baby girl, and my life was filled with immense joy. A year-and-a-half later, our son was born, and now — as you can see — I'm expecting our third child, and I am almost forty-six years old, Mrs. Shain! My husband wanted to give me a treat, and so we came for a short visit to Israel before the birth. Our older children volunteered to take care of the little ones. They and I have grown very close to each other, and they encouraged us to take this vacation together.

Millie paused for a few minutes, and I could see she was choosing her words carefully. "Mrs. Shain, I realize that Hashem has sent me His special blessing in giving me a family at my age; perhaps it is because I accepted His decree that we remain childless during my first marriage, without voicing any complaint and never divulging to anyone that I was not at fault. I hope that my story will bring encouragement to your readers, and be a source of hope."

Millie asked me to use a pseudonym for her name, and I changed the situation a bit, in order to protect her privacy, but the message is unchangeable....

❊ ❊ ❊

Many years ago, I worked as the executive secretary for a religious, charitable institution. There were five other secretaries, and since I was the oldest, they often shared their problems with me, and I tried to be helpful. They were all young married women with growing families, except for Betty, who had been married for almost five years and still had no children.

One morning I got to the office very early, and found Betty already seated at her desk busily typing. I greeted her, and she looked up at me with a tear-stained face, but I made no remark. As I prepared my work for the day, Betty suddenly said to me, "Mrs. Shain, today is my fifth wedding anniversary, and we still have no children." I knew that Betty had been going for all kinds of medical tests and treatments, and I knew how difficult such a time could be. I too had gone through such a discouraging period when my oldest son was almost eight years old and I had not yet had other children, so I understood her very well.

Instead of offering her the usual words of comfort, though, I said sharply, "Listen, Betty, don't you come complaining to me when your babies keep you up at night — I won't have any pity on you at all!" Her face brightened considerably, and she came over and gave me a big hug. A year passed, and Betty started to have babies — one after the other. After she had left our office, we kept in touch and, of course, I attended all her simchas.

A few years ago, early in the morning on *Erev Shavuos*, there was a knock at my door. I was surprised to see Betty standing there with a few of her children, and I greeted her happily. She gave me a big hug, and took a large pan out of her shopping basket and handed it to me — a luscious cheese cake covered with cherries, for the Festival. "Betty, how did you find time for this?" I asked. "Mrs. Shain," she said accusingly but with a twinkle in her eye, "it wasn't easy, and it's all your fault! I don't want to complain, but my twins are keeping me up at night!"

## Deliverance from Heaven

❀ ❀ ❀

The following story goes back forty years. Yona was a very close friend of mine, who lived in another town. One evening I got a phone call from her sister, who sounded upset. "Yona gave birth to a boy this morning," she told me, "but he's not a normal baby, and we can't calm her down." "What's wrong with him?" I asked. This was her fifth child, and all the others had been normal, healthy children. "He's mongoloid," she said. (In those days, the correct term, Down's Syndrome, was not used by laymen.)

I decided to visit Yona in the hospital. It was a whole day's bus trip, and when I arrived the next afternoon, I found her lying despondently in bed, red-eyed and staring into space. I ran over to her, kissed her, and sat down next to the bed. I held her hand without saying anything. Yona suddenly burst out crying. "Racoma, what am I going to do with such a child? I don't know how the other children will take to him, and I'm wondering if I should bring him home or put him in an institution right away."

After a few minutes, I said quietly, "Yona, I realize what you are going through, but I want you to know that I'm acquainted with several families who have such children, and the families have adjusted very well. They say that these children have an especially lovable character." Yona did not reply, but I could tell that she was taking my words very seriously.

Yona did take her baby home, and at his bris they named him "Chaim" — which means "life." Her husband and the other children grew attached to him right away and showed him loving attention, and Yona also learned to accept the situation. He was a sweet child, who progressed slowly and attended a special school that catered to Down's Syndrome children.

Many years passed, and Yona's children all married, except

of course for Chaim. He had little jobs from time to time, but mostly he stayed at home. Several years ago, Yona's husband had a sudden heart attack and passed away, and she was left at home with Chaim. Since I settled in Jerusalem, we have kept up a close correspondence, and we have met whenever I visited the States.

Her last letter, which I received a few days ago, reads as follows:

Dear Racoma,

Today is Chaim's birthday — he is forty years old. I look back at the day he was born, when it seemed that a dark cloud hovered over me, and I would never see the light again. Now I thank Hashem each day for giving me Chaim — "life" — for my son is truly the one who is giving me the will to live. Since Hershel passed away, and I fractured my leg, I need someone to really be at my side. Chaim, with his cheerful smile, and his readiness to help me, is a great blessing. I see now that Hashem sends His blessings in different ways, but we are too human to understand His great kindness to us.

All my love to you,
Yona

❀ ❀ ❀

Sara introduced herself over the phone. "I know you through your books, Mrs. Shain, and I felt you would understand my situation. I am having a very difficult pregnancy, with twins, and I need prayers and encouragement to get through the next several months."

Of course, I kept in touch with her and prayed for her and for her twins. I tried to give her as much encouragement as I could. After Sara had given birth and recuperated, I asked her to write up her unusual experience for my new book. She graciously agreed and she and her husband, Shmuel, came to visit and brought me their story:

"DO YOU HAVE twins in your family?" asked the ultrasound technician. "No," I answered, assuming that it was another routine question. "Well," she said, "you're expecting twins!"

Shmuel and I left the ultrasound laboratory with mixed feelings. On the one hand, there was the excitement of a double blessing, but on the other hand, I would need to be more careful as the pregnancy progressed, and I wondered how we would cope as our family of four children became six children at one time.

Throughout the first half of the pregnancy all seemed normal. Then in the 20th week, the ultrasound showed that only one of the twins had developed according to the gestational age, while the second one was at least three weeks behind in size. A specialist was called in and after close examination of the ultrasound, diagnosed "stuck twin syndrome." He told me to see my obstetrician as soon as possible.

Shmuel and I were frightened. What did this strange term mean? I prayed that the ultrasound was a faulty one, for I had heard that at times there were mistakes. However, when we saw my obstetrician, and he checked the ultrasound, he took it very seriously, and even sent us for a second opinion to a top-notch specialist in ultrasound techniques. The diagnosis was confirmed, and we realized that my regular twin pregnancy was not going to be regular at all.

The doctor explained to us exactly what we were facing. Twin A was indeed the right size according to the months of development, but twin B was by now clearly falling behind. It seems twin B was supplying twin A with his own blood, via their respective umbilical cords. As the amount of amniotic fluid around the baby is a function of the baby's blood supply, it turned out that while twin A was suffering from too much fluid, twin B had barely any fluid around him. This condition was called twin-to-twin transfusion syndrome, and can only occur with identical twins. It was also complicated because twin B was "stuck" in a corner, where he could not move or grow, because twin A was pressing against him with his ever growing amniotic sac. The prognosis was that since this condition was occurring so early in their development, it meant very little chance of survival for either twin. It seemed that only a miracle could save even one.

Research on this kind of pregnancy was only about ten years old, we were told, and the only medical treatment available was to draw off the excess amniotic fluid from twin A to lessen the pressure on twin B. This could, perhaps, improve the condition, and at least prolong their lives to the extent that either one or both could be born as viable premature babies.

We were confused. Hashem had given us a double blessing with my pregnancy of twins, but now it seemed all was in jeopardy, if not already hopeless. The doctor calmed us down, saying, "As long as there is life, there is hope." He did tell us though that the treatment was a risky one, as it could bring on contractions and induce premature birth. It sounded like a no-win situation. Doing nothing spelled almost certain disaster, but having the series of treatments was definitely risky. We didn't know whether we'd be having two, one, or no babies.

We decided to consult some *Gedolim*, and follow whatever they advised. The Rabbis we consulted were of the opinion that we should undertake the treatments, and they all told us they would pray for me and my twins. We felt more encouraged, and for the first time we had a sense of comfort and faith that Hashem would answer our prayers.

I needed five of the treatments, and each time there was

the chance that the pregnancy would be terminated. However, I went through all of them, and the babies were still alive. My life had undergone a complete change, and I still had to find the emotional and physical strength to be a caring mother to my four young children, who could not understand why Mommy was always "sick."

When I had finished my sixth month, we became more hopeful that the "two, one, or none" might even be two, but the doctors were still very wary of the outcome. Twin A was progressing, but twin B was rapidly losing strength. However, our faith in Hashem was strong, and we faced each day with renewed hope.

I had just about finished my seventh month when I went into labor. When I arrived at the hospital, my doctor, the staff, and a pediatrician were already waiting for me. The caesarean operation had to be performed immediately.

Through the blurriness of the anesthesia, I kept repeating the verse that one of the Rabbis had told me to say: "But you that did cleave unto the Lord your God are alive every one of you this day" (*Devarim* 4:4).

Suddenly, through the haze, I heard my doctor call me as if from afar: "Here's the small one (twin B) — listen to him cry!" By the time twin A was born, I was too sedated to recall anything.

In the recovery room, I was told excitedly that I had given birth to two boys. Twin A weighed about a kilogram and a half, while twin B was way under one kilogram. Both babies had survived! The next morning, the doctor informed me that twin A was doing fine, but twin B was very weak....

Twin B lived for 29 hours, and then gave up the fight, but Hashem saved twin A for us. He needed a lot of special care, and I saw him through his maze of tubes every day. He was hospitalized for five weeks, and at the age of two-and-a-half months he was able to have his bris.

We thank Hashem for giving us the inner strength to face the trials of this time and our loss, and for giving us the clarity of mind to see His kindness throughout the entire period. Though twin B did not survive, we are still thankful to Hashem that I gave birth to two live babies, and that I heard twin B give his first cry. He clearly was not meant to spend much time in this world. His life's purpose had been fulfilled during his few prenatal months and his short existence in the world.

Shmuel and I don't claim to understand the possible reasons for this unusual pregnancy, but we feel that our prayers have not been in vain. The verse says: "The secret things belong to the Lord our God, but the things that are revealed belong to us and to our children forever, that we may do all the words of this Torah" (*Devarim* 29:28).

❃ ❃ ❃

Aaron and Chaya Hinda waited almost four years for the arrival of their first child. They brought him home from the hospital on their fourth wedding anniversary.

When Chaya Hinda was almost due to give birth, she and her husband had discussed names for their baby. Aaron had his heart set on the name "Yoel Moshe" if the baby were a boy. When Chaya Hinda asked him why he wanted this name, he explained, "Moshe is after Rabbi Moshe Feinstein, and Yoel is after the Satmar Rebbe, Rabbi Yoel Teitelbaum, may their memories be for a blessing." Chaya Hinda was quite surprised by his choice; they had known Reb Moshe, but hadn't had any previous connection with the Satmar Rebbe. "I can't explain why I want the name 'Yoel' so much," Aaron told her, "but the feeling is very strong." When she saw that it meant so much to her husband, Chaya Hinda agreed to the name.

She did give birth to a boy — two weeks after the expected time — and they waited anxiously for the bris. Their son was named "Yoel Moshe," just as Aaron had so much wanted. After the bris, a smiling Aaron came over to Chaya Hinda and said excitedly, "One of the rabbis just told me that today, the twenty-sixth of Av, is the Satmar Rebbe's *yahrtzeit!*"

Now Aaron and Chaya Hinda understood the attachment to the name, and even why she had given birth two weeks late.

"Our *emunah* was strengthened as we merited knowing why this name was chosen for our son," she told me. "May our Yoel Moshe emulate these two great Torah giants."

❊ ❊ ❊

It is very rewarding for me to include the story of my close friends Leah and Sandy David in this chapter. I have used pseudonyms for some of the people in this story. Leah writes:

*It is now past midnight, and Gittel Bracha David is fast asleep. She will be eight weeks old tomorrow. She was born on July 5, 1995, at 2:17 PM, the 7th of Tammuz at Lenox Hill Hospital, in Manhattan, by caesarean section. Her first cry resounded through the delivery room and entered my heart, and I gave thanks to Hashem for this very special Bracha that He sent to Sandy and me.*

*How many tears have I shed from the countless disappointments of infertility and the involved fertility treatments over the past seven years! Seven years is a long time to look forward to a baby, especially at my age — I was 36 years old when we got married. Yes, there was a lot of pain, but there was also always the hope that Hashem would answer our prayers, and the prayers of all our loved ones who were praying for us.*

On March 19, 1988 — the second of Nisan — Sandy and I were married. I am a *ba'alas teshuvah*, and it was not long after I decided to live a life of Torah and mitzvos that Sandy and I met. We hoped we would be blessed with a large family, but when a year had almost passed since the wedding and I was still not expecting, I sought the advice of a doctor. Since I was almost 37 years old then, and Sandy was two years older, we were both anxious and a little worried that our family had not yet begun.

The doctor informed me that I had a problem that probably was preventing me from becoming pregnant and advised me to undergo treatment to correct it. After three months, when the problem was considered cured, our hopes rose again.

After months went by and our hopes were not realized, I went to a well-known fertility specialist, who suggested two options for further treatment. Both were very expensive, time consuming, and physically taxing.

Sandy and I opted for the one that was "easier," but still kept me on an emotional roller-coaster, as my hopes rose and fell after each treatment. It was a time of tears for me, and left both of us in despair, although we tried our best to keep up our spirits and continued to pray that Hashem answer our pleas.

Next, we tried the more complicated procedure, and once again, began a period of great strain which drained me emotionally and drained our budget as well — one treatment could cost between $5,000 and $10,000! After unsuccessful treatments, Sandy and I decided that we needed a break, and we planned a trip to Israel.

When we arrived, we ran from one holy place to the other, and at each stop, our prayers were the same: "Please, Hashem, answer our prayers and bless us with a child." I lit candles all over Israel, and my tears wet the graves of many *tzaddikim*. We were introduced to a special guide, who understood our situation. He suggested that we visit a very great man, a revered *mekubal,* and ask him for his advice and blessing.

We drove for three hours to the mystic's house, which was packed with people waiting to see him. When our turn finally came, our guide served as translator.

The *mekubal* gave us a blessing for having children, and then advised me to do three things: 1) Do everything medically possible, 2) cook or bake food for a *tzaddik*, and 3) take an orphan into our home. We decided we would try to fulfill his advice.

When we returned to New York, I once again contacted the fertility specialist. Undergoing the procedure entailed traveling out of town, and since there was a heavy snowstorm that day, and the train almost broke down, I thought I wouldn't make it — but I did. It also meant returning on a particular day a few days later to complete the procedure. This fell on a Friday. I started out at 5:00 AM, again in a howling snowstorm, caught a train, and then a car service to the doctor's office. When I walked in, the receptionist stared at me as if I had come from Mars. "How did you make it all the way here from New York?" she gasped. I returned home just an hour before candle lighting, exhausted beyond description. When it became clear that the treatment had not succeeded, we decided to take a break and go on to the other things we had been advised to do.

I'd heard about a great Rabbi from Israel who had just arrived in New York, and after inquiries I found out where he was staying. I called up his hosts and asked if I could bake challos for the Rabbi for the coming Shabbos, and I explained why this meant so much to me. The lady of the house readily agreed, and so each Friday, for as long as the Rabbi was in New York, I baked two large challos and brought them to him.

Now I had fulfilled two of the *mekubal*'s suggestions, and it left only the third — to bring an orphan into our home.

We decided to look into adoption possibilities and went full steam ahead. I figured that if Hashem does not want us to have our own children, perhaps we were meant to adopt a child. I wrote the following letter to forty-five Jewish family service agencies across the country. The letter was dated March 14, 1994 — almost six years to the day since our marriage:

> Dear Friend,
> Imagine a warm, loving, secure Jewish home. A garden that grows in the spring. Challah baking in the oven for the Sabbath — but still the Sabbath table is empty. No laughing, no crying, no sharing, no building memories. There are only empty chairs waiting to be filled, and maybe you and your organization can help.
> I am a young 42-year-old and my husband is a young 44-year-old. We are both stable, intelligent, sensitive professionals. We own our home and are established in our community. We have been hoping for a child of our own since we married six years ago, but unfortunately this has not happened. We have come to realize that the important issue is to become parents even if the child or children are not our very own.
> We are interested in adopting white, healthy children, from newborn infants until age seven. We would consider more than one child. I am sure that our new family is out there someplace just waiting to come home. Please think of us when the next infant or child needs a real home!!
> We can supply references upon request. Please contact us about what our next steps should be.
> Sincerely yours,
> Leah David,
> long-waiting mother....

The letter did very well, as I received 30 responses and 10 phone calls...but no children. I also tried to contact standard adoption agencies as well as foreign agencies, lawyers, and some Rabbis who were knowledgeable in this area. I felt there must be a baby waiting for us, and I did not want to keep it waiting too long!

All my relatives and friends had children, and I began to feel as if Sandy and I were the only people in the world who weren't having babies. Someone told me a story about two women, both childless, who went to a great Rebbe in Europe to ask for a blessing. A year later one of them had a baby, but the other did not. The second one returned to the Rebbe and asked why she did not merit as her friend had, since they were both given the same blessing. The Rebbe replied, "You were both given the same blessing, but did you see what she did last year? She walked around with an empty baby carriage, because she had absolute faith that her prayers would be answered."

This story hit home, and since I had been knitting outfits for all my friends' babies, I proceeded to knit a sweater for my own little girl. When people asked me who I was knitting for this time, I answered simply, "For my future daughter." This was the empty baby carriage that I had heard about in the story.

A few weeks later, I saw an ad in the news: "Urgently needed. A loving, secure, warm home in the New York area for a 12-year-old girl." I took a deep breath and called. I spoke to the Rabbi handling the case, described our home, and told him that we would be happy to take care of this girl. I learned that she was an orphan who had lost her father not long ago, and her mother was too ill to care for her. Sandy and I were chosen to have this orphan girl as a foster child. In fact, the Rabbi said that the reason we were chosen from all the many qualified people who responded to the ad was that we were the only ones who did not ask first about financial compensation and adoption. In other words, we had shown interest only in the child herself.

Taking our foster daughter in was the most challenging experience in our lives. It changed us for the better, though it was not always easy for us or for her. I felt that finally we had done the three things the *mekubal* in Israel had advised us to do. Our foster daughter stayed with us for two months until her mother's health improved and she was able to care for her again.

A few months later, one of the girls in my office mentioned that she had a very fine gynecologist. She told me that Dr. Jacobs took a genuine personal interest in each of his patients. Since I felt it was time for a check-up anyway, I made an appointment.

I was a new patient, and he had a long consultation with me. He was interested in hearing my complete case history. I related my entire sorrowful story, all the treatments and procedures I had gone through, all my hopes and disappointments. I used up a half a box of tissues wiping the tears from my eyes. When I finished, he said simply, "You still want to have a baby, don't you?"

"Of course I do," I wept, "but it seems I can't."

"This may surprise you," the doctor said. "I think that your problem is relatively minor and that I can help you, Leah. I will prescribe a plain bottle of cough syrup. I realize that this sounds ridiculously simple after all the sophisticated and expensive treatments you've gone through, but this cough syrup can cause changes not only in the upper respiratory tract. You can buy it over the counter and it costs just a few dollars." He then wrote out his instructions for when I should take it and how much I should take.

I left Dr. Jacobs' office thinking he was absolutely crazy. We had spent thousands of dollars and I'd gone through excruciating tests and treatments without any results — and now a few spoonfuls of cough syrup taken on certain days would help me have a baby? I decided not to tell Sandy or anyone else about this — it was just too ridiculous. However, the girl in my office who had recommended Dr. Jacobs to me, kept asking me what he had advised, and I finally broke down and told her. "What have you got to lose?" she said. "It will cost you only a few dollars and a few spoonfuls of cough syrup."

On my way home from work that day, I felt a strong pull to park my car when I passed a drug store. I gave in to that feeling, went in, and bought the cough syrup. I hadn't decided to take it, but at least, I told myself, I'll have it in the house if I need it for a cough! Of course, when I got home, I took a teaspoon of it, and since it was not bad-tasting at all, I thought, Well, why not? So I started to take the cough syrup at the special times the doctor had designated, still telling myself he must be a little crazy.

Two months later, I began to have signs and symptoms but I was sure they meant nothing, so I sat back and waited. I had been taking the cough medicine, and had even confided in Sandy about it. He agreed with me that the doctor must be a strange fellow!

When more time had passed and the symptoms wouldn't go away, I called Dr. Jacobs, and he said, "Go and take a pregnancy test, and call me back."

"I'm not pregnant," I half-shrieked at him, "and I can't bear to go through all the disappointment again!" However, when I put down the phone, I went to the nearest drug store — against my better judgment — bought the special kit for testing pregnancy, and put it into my purse.

Dr. Jacobs would not let it go! His nurse called me the next morning at work to find out what the test had shown. When I told her that I hadn't done it, she said, "Dr. Jacobs insists that you do so. Please give us the result as soon as you have it."

I followed my doctor's orders, and waited. I knew that the

true results take a full five minutes to show up.

The positive sign showed up immediately, but I was sure there was some mistake, and it would soon turn to a negative. So I waited and counted the seconds with my heart thumping wildly. No, it wasn't changing. "Oh! Oh! It can't be," I whispered to myself over and over again, but the positive sign remained. I ran to the phone and called the nurse. "It's positive!" I cried.

"Come in tomorrow morning then, to see Dr. Jacobs," she said with a lilt in her voice. I hung up and kept whispering over and over, "I'm going to have a baby! *Baruch Hashem! Baruch Hashem!*"

I called Sandy and told him. "Go home right now and lie down!" he cried. "Don't talk to anyone! I'll be home right away!"

The next day, the doctor confirmed that I was truly pregnant. The following months were the most wonderful, happiest time of our lives. I loved every minute, from buying maternity clothes to having heartburn! Each sonogram was a special thrill as the baby grew and grew and grew.

All our relatives and friends were thrilled with the wonderful news. I called my friends in Israel, and they, too, shared our great joy through the wires, which seemed to sing along with the delightful news. I was given advice by everyone: "Don't strain yourself; don't pick up anything heavy; don't get fatigued...." It was all music to my ears.

No matter how difficult the past seven years had been, I had always found solace in the last sentence of the first paragraph of *Hallel*: "He causes the barren woman of the house to sit as a joyous mother of children, *Halleluyah!*" (*Tehillim* 113:9).

Thank you, Hashem! Thank you, Sandy! Thank you, Dr. Jacobs! Thank you, all our loved ones who shared our sorrow and joy.

*"Good night, Gittel Bracha. Mommy loves you...."*

❀ ❀ ❀

*Author's note:*
Leah's story covered forty typewritten pages, as she detailed her many tests and treatments. I edited her manuscript, but tried to make sure as I wrote that the reader would experience some of what Leah endured in her long and anxious road toward motherhood.

❀ ❀ ❀

Although the birth of a baby usually brings great joy, it can also happen that a newborn baby comes into the world with many problems, and the parents suffer pain and must be strong in their faith to learn to cope. Yaffa sent me her touching account of how she tries to overcome the pain and find peace of mind in her difficult situation:

DARKNESS! That is the word which describes our feelings when we heard that there was something wrong with our newborn baby. Little Raizy had a very rare syndrome, one of the major symptoms of which was seizures. She was taken for CT scans, EEGs, blood tests, and ECHOgrams. She was attached to various machines that recorded numbers and squiggly lines and important information.

Right after birth, many mothers feel oversensitive and weepy, and I did too. I recall that even before I was given the disturbing news about my baby, I lay in bed and cried. Was it a quick post-partum depression, a natural hormonal reaction, or did I somehow sense that something was wrong? An hour later, when the doctor told me the news, I realized that now I really did have something to cry about, and darkness seemed to descend on me.

The hospital arranged meetings for us with neonatal pediatricians, neurologists, and a social worker. During the meetings, many thoughts and questions filled my mind, but the major one was: "How will I handle this?" Following that, came: "How will I take care of my other children when I have this very sick child?" It seemed like a nightmare that had become very real.

Hashem gives us many trials in our lives that we are capable of handling. I tried to believe that I was stronger than I thought, and I looked for courage to face the future. However, I was very frightened, as I realized my life had changed forever. My family and friends gave me moral support, and showed their concern. Since my family does not live close to me, I had to rely on long-distance phone calls from them. I was worried about how my mother would react, but she turned out to be one of my greatest sources of encouragement, anticipating what the psychologists and social workers advised.

The doctors told us that we would be able to take our baby home as soon as the right medication was found for controlling her seizures. After seven weeks and many medications, they told us that they had done all they could, but the seizures continued. So we brought Raizy home, and she had from ten to twenty seizures daily. Fortunately, this did not require any special care except oral medication.

Her motor development was very delayed, so I began to take her for physiotherapy several times a week. This was difficult to manage, and when Raizy was seven months old, we found a special day-care center for her where she received all her therapies, plus warm and loving care. She was taken by transportation each morning and brought home at 3:30 PM. I was very thankful that I could finally have more time for my husband and my other children, and still know that little Raizy was getting everything she needed and even more than I could give her at home.

A friend asked me if our home had changed since Raizy's birth. I posed the question to one of my daughters. "Oh, yes," she said. "It's much nicer having this cutie around!"

On another occasion, I pointed out to my five-year-old son, Shlomo, that a little girl who was running around near our house was in fact the same age as our Raizy. He looked at me, wide-eyed, and exclaimed, "How can that be? Raizy's just a baby."

I was quiet for a moment then I said, "You know, Shlomo, that your sister may not — God forbid — ever walk. Would you love her anyway?"

"Of course!" he replied. "I would love her even more!"

Efrat, my oldest daughter, is twelve years old, and is very close to Raizy. Once I asked her, "When you look at other babies, do you feel bad? What do you think when you see them? Does it hurt you when you compare Raizy to them?" Efrat did not understand why I should ask such a thing. "What do you mean, Imma?" she said. "I just remember that Hashem made Raizy like she is and the other babies like they are."

My eight-year-old, Nechami, was on the porch with one of her little friends, Leah. I heard Leah telling her all about her own little brother, what he does, how he's beginning to talk, etc. "Our baby doesn't do anything," I heard Nechami say. Then she added, "My mother went to a Rav, and he told her that our baby's *neshamah* is very holy, and that Hashem chose us — our family — to take care of this special baby."

"Really?" Leah asked, in awe.

"Yes, really!" Nechami replied proudly.

I stood there, listening to the conversation and thanking Hashem that my children were learning at a young age that being different is nothing to be ashamed of. When I told my son, Shlomo, that his prayers for Raizy were dear to Hashem, he answered, simply, "Yes, Imma, children are holy like a *sefer*, but children like Raizy are holy like a *sefer Torah*!" I continue to listen to my children's words and draw strength and courage from them.

As Raizy's first birthday approached, I felt thankful that the year had passed and that she was doing more than we had expected. Although, to an onlooker, it may not have seemed very much, to us every tiny bit of progress was cause for us to celebrate, and to thank Hashem. A friend of mine organized a party in honor of Raizy's birthday. It would be a different kind of party — a gathering for reciting *Tehillim*. When I arrived at Rachel's home with Raizy, twenty of my friends were awaiting us with their *Tehillim* in their hands. We recited much of the *Tehillim* as Raizy sat in her stroller in the center, wearing the crown her sisters had made her for her birthday. Before leaving, a heart-shaped cake was served. It was decorated with the words, "*Mazal tov*, Raizy. We love you!"

My oldest daughter decided that she too wanted to make a special meeting of her Shabbat *Tehillim* group for Raizy's birthday, so Raizy was again surrounded by girls praying for her recovery. I am sure that all those prayers helped my precious daughter. I know they helped me.

That week, I also brought a birthday cake to the staff of the day-care center. They had decorated Raizy's special chair and made her a floral crown in honor of the day. I thanked each member of the staff for their loving and caring attention, and added, "All of you who have chosen to work here are very special people. You give and give of yourselves with love and dedication to further each child's progress. It is truly a privilege to know you." I then mentioned that a doctor had once referred to my daughter as a pitiful child. "I invite him here today to see the staff who love Raizy and work so diligently to help her progress."

Now that Raizy is almost two years old, we cannot think of her as being associated with the word "darkness." Her shining eyes and bright disposition bring light into our home. Our sweet little girl, whom we once thought had brought darkness into our lives, now is the one who radiates a shining light to all who surround her. Things are not always easy, but I know that if Hashem brought Raizy into this world, surely He had His reasons for creating her the way she is. When I find myself worrying about her progress and about what the future holds, I remember with firm faith that just as Hashem has helped us today, He will help us tomorrow....

❊ ❊ ❊

MALKA AND DOV HAD been married for almost fourteen years, and were still, to their great sorrow, childless. The fertility problem was Dov's, and he had gone through many tests, treatments, and procedures at the hand of expert specialists, to no avail!

One day when they were visiting their Rebbe, and their pain, sorrow, and discouragement were evident, he gave them a blessing: They would have a child within the year! Stunned and puzzled, they nevertheless had complete faith that if the Rebbe gave them this blessing, it would surely come true.

At that time, Dov was teaching in a special yeshiva program for *ba'alei teshuvah*, which had a private tutoring program to help the newcomers study Gemara. He would teach a student for several months until he was advanced enough in his learning to join the regular *shiur* and then Dov would begin with another student.

Dov's newest student was a young man who had traveled throughout the world trying to "find himself." He had finally decided that in becoming an observant Jew and studying Torah he would find what he was searching for, and now he was settling down to learn. He told Dov that he had been in the Far East, where he had studied Oriental medicine, namely herbal medicine and acupuncture.

The two men became very friendly and one day Dov decided to mention his problem and ask if Oriental medicine could help.

The young man nodded. "Possibly," he said. "You see, Western medicine and Oriental medicine are very different from each other. Their respective approaches to diagnosis and treatment reflect the different ways in which they understand the workings of the body, and the basis of health and illness.

"I think I might be able to help you, Dov," he concluded. "It's certainly worth a try."

He gave Dov various herbs to eat, and started him on acupuncture treatments. Within a few months, the Rebbe's blessing actualized and they learned that Malka was expecting their first child. At the time of this writing, they have been blessed with four lovely children.

*Chazal* say: "When a *tzaddik* gives a blessing on earth, Hashem sanctions it in Heaven."

❊ ❊ ❊

MENDEL HAD BEEN married for almost four years and he and his wife still had no children. His close friend, Label, had just become the father of triplet boys after he and his wife had themselves been childless for several years. On Purim, Label came to visit Mendel and told him, "Last year, I received a *berachah* from the Rebbe and, *baruch Hashem*, our prayers were answered. They say that Purim is a very special day, a day when prayers are accepted by Hashem. Since it's Purim today, let's go to the Rebbe together and ask him for a blessing for you and your wife too."

Mendel agreed and they set out, but they found the *beis midrash* so packed with all the Rebbe's *chasidim* that there was no way for the two to even get near the Rebbe. Mendel was disappointed, but Label did not give up. He tried frantically to attract the Rebbe's attention by waving his arms to and fro, and fortunately, both Label and Mendel were very tall young men.

Finally, the Rebbe noticed them, and Label, pointing to Mendel, made a sign with three fingers hoping the Rebbe would understand and give Mendel a blessing for triplets! Mendel, however, held up only one finger, modestly hoping that the Rebbe would give him a blessing for at least one child!

The Rebbe looked at Mendel with his concentrated gaze for a minute or two, and then held up two of his own fingers! When Purim came around the following year, Mendel's wife had given birth to twin boys.

# The Long Journey Home

THOSE WHO HAVE DWELT IN THE LAND OF DARKNESS, UPON THEM HAS THE LIGHT SHONE. (YESHAYAHU 9:1)

ALTHOUGH ANNE'S FAMILY was Jewish, they lived a completely secular and assimilated life in a California town near the ocean. Even as a child, she was different from her siblings and her friends. She had a very strong sense of justice, would not tell even little "white" lies, and refused to watch television programs that contained immoral behavior. Her family ridiculed her and called her a "prude." In her junior high school, children dated at the age of thirteen and drugs were already being sold nearby. She began to keep completely to herself, and was looked upon as a loner as well as a prude.

When her family went to the beach, she refused to join them because she felt immodest there. Her sisters and brother laughed at her, and one summer morning when they were preparing to go to the beach, her mother said to her, "Since you never come with us, why don't you go find yourself a job so you'll have something to do!"

Anne took her mother's comment seriously, made signs saying she was interested in babysitting jobs, and placed them in some adjoining apartment buildings. Within a few days she had a job babysitting three mornings a week for the Cohens. Mrs. Cohen was a religious woman, whose husband was a teacher in the yeshiva a few miles away.

And so as Anne started her babysitting job, a new life opened up for her. She was fascinated by the Cohens' behavior, by their practices, by their whole way of life. They themselves took a great liking to Anne, and began to invite her for Shabbos meals. Slowly, she began to gravitate to their life style and to want to make it hers.

By the time Anne graduated from high school, she had decided to keep Shabbos in her home as best as she could, and not to eat anything that was not kosher. She bought herself some plastic dishes and shopped in the supermarket for kosher items. Her parents were offended and angry and one Shabbos when Anne refused to turn off the light in her room, her mother shouted, "I've had enough of your religious, fanatical nonsense. Either you become normal again, or you can find another place to live!"

Anne quickly packed a few of her clothes and ran to the Cohens' home. Tearfully she told them how miserable she had been for years, and how her mother had now given her an ultimatum. "I never want to go back!" she cried.

The Cohens realized that Anne needed sensitive and understanding care as well as a practical solution. She was on her own now and would never return to her parents' home. Since they had family in Israel who were involved in various study programs for American girls, they suggested the idea to Anne, who eagerly accepted the opportunity.

Anne was welcomed warmly by the Cohen cousins, who were originally from the United States themselves. She began to attend a seminary for *ba'alei teshuvah*, and in no time, Anne became a truly religious girl. Her past began to fade like a bad dream, and she found great joy and solace in her new life in Israel.

Her parents wrote and phoned, and kept trying to convince her to come home and become a "normal girl" again. But Anne had no intention of ever returning to her "home" or to her previous life. She had found a new and better home. Her parents finally made peace with the situation when they realized that Anne was adamant.

Several years passed, and Anne was introduced to a fine young man who was studying in a yeshiva. He too came from the United States and they were very suited to each other. Their wedding was a particularly joyous one.

Today Anne — who has been Chana for several years — has a wonderful family and her children are growing up in a Jewish home of Torah and mitzvos. It was a long, difficult road that she followed, but it brought her to her true home....

❀ ❀ ❀

SHIRLEY WAS BORN and raised in South Africa. Her family was somewhat traditional; her mother lit candles on Friday nights, and her father went to synagogue on Saturday mornings. Shirley had no formal Jewish education however, and the main interest in her life was sports.

She was an avid hockey player and one day, when she was sixteen, she twisted her knee while playing hockey and suffered excruciating pain. She had torn her cartilage, and would need minor surgery.

The surgery proved more complicated than expected, and Shirley needed physiotherapy afterwards. As a result, she became so interested in physiotherapy, that she decided to become a physiotherapist herself. By the time she enrolled at the university for the full four-year course, her knee had healed sufficiently to allow her to return to her sports.

In her third year of studies, Shirley injured the same knee

while she was playing hockey, and this time her doctor told her she would probably never play hockey again. She was devastated, but began to seek comfort in music, which she always enjoyed. She took piano lessons from a very fine teacher, a religious woman, who imparted to Shirley a deep awareness of her Jewish heritage along with the music she was teaching her. As a result, Shirley began to learn more about Judaism and she decided to take a trip to Israel, where she had never been, and to visit her parents' cousins in Jerusalem. They were a religious family, and Shirley's stay in Israel drew her even closer to her Jewish roots.

By the time she returned to South Africa, Shirley was a different person, a committed Jewess who aspired to live a religious life. Some time later she met her future husband, who was also a *ba'al teshuvah*. After they were married, they decided to settle in Israel, where they have been blessed with a lovely family.

Shirley asked me to end her story with the following:

"When I injured my knee and was told that I could never take part in sports again, I was very depressed and thought it was the greatest tragedy. Little did I know that our Father in Heaven was planning an entirely new life for me, which has given me the ultimate in true happiness and spiritual fulfillment."

❀ ❀ ❀

LEAH WAS BORN IN Westphalia, Germany, one of a family of six children. When the Second World War broke out, she was four years old. As the war intensified, her parents arranged to send Leah and two older sisters to London on the *Kindertransport*. And so little Leah and her sisters were destined to live, while her brother, two other sisters, and her mother were sent to a concentration camp and killed.

Her father, a *shochet*, was young, healthy, and strong; he was sent to a work camp where he remained for five years until he was liberated after the war. Desperate to find his three surviving children, he succeeded in tracing them and set out for London.

Leah and her sisters had been transferred from one hostel to another as the war had come closer to London. They had suffered greatly from the separation from their family and from everything they knew. They were among the few religious children in the hostel, and in time, they forgot their background and simply became Jewish refugees far from their family and home.

When Leah's father arrived in London, he had not seen his children for almost seven years. He stood facing his three daughters who seemed and acted as strangers to him. However, he immediately took them under his care. Within a year he remarried, and Leah and her sisters had to cope not only with a father trying to bring them back to *Yiddishkeit*, but with a stepmother as well. It was difficult for them all.

Leah's father was exacting in his demands that his daughters become religious girls once again. He enrolled them in a school where all the students came from Orthodox homes. His perseverance bore fruit, however, and slowly they made the long journey back to their Jewish heritage.

Now, many years later, Leah and her husband have been blessed with children and grandchildren who are all on the path of Torah. She looks back with thankfulness to Hashem not only because she and her sisters remained alive, but also because He saved them and their descendants from being lost to our Jewish Nation.

❦ ❦ ❦

The following experience was told to me by someone who

wishes to remain anonymous.

ON THE LAST EVENING of Chanukah, I took a walk through our Jerusalem neighborhood with my three youngest children. The windows and entranceways glowed with the lights of Chanukah. On street after street, in all directions, my children pointed with delight at each menorah proudly announcing the miracles of Chanukah. What my beloved children did not notice was the wistful expression on my face.

I grew up in a small town in America. My next-door neighbors were religious Dutch Lutherans; directly across the street was a German family; they had an Irish family on one side and an Italian family on the other. Even our telephone number reflected our gentile neighborhood: Chapel 9-2124.

Like the three other Jewish families on our street, we had a Chanukah menorah, which we lit on our dining room table. During the "holiday season" all our neighbors' homes had their doors and windows fully decorated with the traditional wreaths, and with a smiling Santa Claus with his sleigh and reindeer. One of the homes had a miniature manger scene on their front lawn. Night after night carolers would go from house to house singing their religious songs. Chanukah always seemed so mundane to me compared to the lavish celebrations of our neighbors. I remember dreading being asked "what I got for Chanukah," and always exaggerating to compete with my friends!

Despite our religious differences, though, we were all good friends. Although my father made sure that we knew we were Jewish, our observance of Jewish tradition was more cultural than religious. Thus, while I was keenly aware that I was different from my gentile friends, I never expressed these feelings.

In school, I was an active and popular student. I acted as if I were one of the crowd, and because it was important for me to be accepted, I made sure to have the right friends and the right look. Fitting in meant keeping my Jewish side — and I wasn't even sure what that really meant — at a very low profile. I must have sensed that my Jewish identity would be a barrier to reaching the "right" social circles.

From my earliest years in school, when we were taught American history, and how America was one great "melting pot" of peoples from all over the world, forging together to make it a strong and enriched country, I was very taken with the idea. I wanted it to be true for me, a Jewish girl, too, that we would forge ahead together, combining our talents and not being judged by race, color, or religion.

When I had graduated from university at the age of 21, I felt unsure about this goal, however. These were the years of student protests, and I wondered if the war in Vietnam was just or not; there were minorities suffering in rich America — shouldn't I get involved in their struggles? I was losing faith in all that I had believed in and felt part of in the years of my childhood and adolescence.

I even explored the keen feeling that there was a God, and searched for ways of reaching Him, but I could not find Him. I looked to my own heritage, but it left me unmoved in its Conservative and Reform expressions.

When I began to practice social work in the Southwest, befriending and assisting poverty-stricken American Indians, my father suggested I help my own people first. But when I looked around, my own people seemed to be achieving the American dream, and did not need my help.

In the early fall of 1973, an old friend from college invited me to visit her for a few days at the University of Michigan at East Lansing, where she was studying for her Doctorate in Political Science. I enjoyed the traditional ivy-covered buildings and tree-lined streets, and it was equally enjoyable to spend time with my old friend. As we sat together in the student cafeteria, we caught up on each other's lives over the past three years. Chris was of German-American ancestry, and I remembered vaguely that her father was rumored to have been a Nazi sympathizer. In those days, I was quite ignorant of Jewish history and had only a superficial knowledge of the German atrocities during the war. Of course, the term "Nazi" had negative connotations for everyone, but I judged my friend and her father by how they treated me and nothing else.

Chris was active in the women's movement. In the early 70s, people were involved in so many causes that nothing surprised me. Every car had a bumper sticker boasting of the driver's particular cause. I never knew if I were talking to a "Save the Whales" person, or a member of a radical political group or a religious cult. Women's lib was one of the most widespread campus movements at that time. My interest in the movement was limited to equal rights for all in the working sector.

While I was visiting Chris, a campus-wide women's lib meeting was scheduled and Chris encouraged me to attend. Why not? I told myself. It should be interesting. And it certainly was.

The meeting was so crowded that Chris and I sat on the floor. I was looking forward to having a good time, and I did not know then that Hashem had turned a "shining light" on me.

The first speaker gave her talk; and then another speaker took the platform and, in her speech, made a reference to "the Judeo-Christian tradition." Suddenly, a woman from the audience stood up and interrupted her: "There is no such thing as a Judeo-Christian tradition! There was a Jewish tradition and there was a Christian tradition, but there could never be a fusion of the two!"

That was it — the meeting which had been intended to foster unity among the female students, disintegrated and broke up into heated discussion groups on the subject. I noticed that Chris was looking me, and when she asked, "Well, what do *you* think?" my heart was beating rapidly. After a momentary hesitation, I blurted out, "I think she's right." Chris frowned. "Who's right?" she asked, just to make sure she understood me. "The woman in the audience. There is no Judeo-Christian tradition," I declared.

In all honesty, I did not know on what I based my affirmation, but once I had said it, I stuck to my position. Something seemed to be happening to me. Deep inside I felt it was true. I was overcome with emotion, and what was more puzzling was that my good friend, Chris, was absolutely livid. She would not speak to me afterwards, and our long-time friendship was over. I left her home and got the first flight back and I never spoke to or heard from her again.

On the plane I tried to make sense of what had happened, but I couldn't. It was raining hard when I arrived in New York. As I drove my car home from the airport, I flipped on the radio, and Hashem intensified the shining light.

The news report announced; "Israel has been attacked on all sides." It was Yom Kippur! All of a sudden, I started to cry as I hadn't cried since I was a child. I couldn't drive. I pulled over to the side of the highway, and just sat in the car, crying. My tears blended in with the pouring rain. "My brothers are dying," I murmured to myself. From my deepest self, I pulled out a Jewish commitment, for the first time in my life. I made sort of a vow, knowing nothing of Halachah, that from this time on, I would not eat anything that was *traif*.

It was more than an act of solidarity with my own people. It was the end of my belief in the melting pot. Something very big had happened that Yom Kippur, something I didn't understand at that moment. I had changed directions and was on my way to a new life....